Our Massachusetts

By Susan Cole Kelly

Voyageur Press

First published in 2005 by Voyageur Press, an imprint of MBI Publishing Company, Galtier Plaza, Suite 200, 380 Jackson Street, St. Paul, MN 55101-3885 USA

Edited by Danielle J. Ibister
Printed in China

05   06   07   08   09   5   4   3   2   1

Library of Congress Cataloging-in-Publication Data

Kelly, Susan Cole, 1950-
  Our Massachusetts / by Susan Cole Kelly.
    p. cm.
  ISBN-13: 978-0-89658-683-3 (hardback)
  ISBN-10: 0-89658-683-9 (hardback)
  1. Historic sites—Massachusetts—Pictorial works. 2. Massachusetts—Pictorial works. 3. Massachusetts—Description and travel. 4. Massachusetts—History, Local—Pictorial works. I. Title.
  F65.K45 2005
  917.44'0022'2—dc22

                            2005009345

Page 1: *Acres of clean white sand and an incomparable view of Cape Cod Bay highlight Mayflower Beach in Dennis.* Cape Cod Life *magazine readers regularly vote Mayflower one of the best beaches on the mid-Cape. Jam-packed with beach umbrellas in August, it is quiet by September.*

Page 2: *Cape Cod juts into the ocean, forcing ships to navigate treacherous waters between New York and Boston. In 1797, the new federal government constructed Highland (Cape Cod) Light, after appeals from the Massachusetts Humane Society, then responsible for saving the lives of shipwrecked passengers and crew.*

Page 3: *The Cape Cod National Seashore was established in 1961 to preserve forty miles of pristine beach as well as such treasures as salt marshes, kettle ponds, woodlands, lighthouses, and historic buildings that demonstrate how people traditionally have lived with the land.*

Page 4: *New Salem's crisp white 1794 Meetinghouse is eclipsed by bright maple trees in autumn. Village commons peppered the countryside in the mid-nineteenth century. Now they serve as treasured reminders of simpler times.*

Page 5: *Fall foliage surrounds the gristmill at Longfellow's Wayside Inn in Sudbury, originally the 1716 Howe's Tavern. The mill was built by automobile magnate Henry Ford, who also built a country church and moved a one-room schoolhouse to the property and then turned it all into a non-profit site.*

Title page, main photo: *America's first botanical garden open to the public, Boston Public Garden includes acres of flowers, hundreds of trees, and a short suspension bridge spanning a manmade lagoon with swan boats. The garden is part of Frederick Law Olmsted's Emerald Necklace, a six-mile chain of parks that stretches from downtown to Dorchester.*

Title page, inset: *The Old South Meeting House served as the departure point of the Boston Tea Party, where revolutionaries calling themselves the Sons of Liberty dumped tea in the harbor to protest British taxes. Members of Old South included Benjamin Franklin, James Otis, and William Dawes.*

Contents page, main photo: *The brick mansions on Nantucket's cobbled Main Street were built during the heyday of the whaling era. Listed on the national historic register, the downtown district exemplifies a thriving whaling town of the 1830s.*

Contents page, inset: *The Middlesex County Volunteers Fifes and Drums entertain at Boston's Harborfest. The week-long festival celebrates the city's colonial and maritime heritage with hundreds of activities, exhibits, reenactments, and tours.*

Dedication

To my mom and my dad. Now I understand how proud they were.

To Jon, for convincing me that I could do it.

To Gary, for challenging me to do it better.

To Anne, the angel who taught me that it does make a difference.

To all the people in all the towns who shared their secret spots with me.

Acknowledgments

The author gratefully acknowledges Jon Marcus, editor of *Boston Magazine*, for reviewing this manuscript, and The Trustees of Reservations for their assistance and advice.

At Gloucester's Rocky Neck Art Colony, a colorful patchwork of art galleries, restaurants, and boutiques, such luminaries as Winslow Homer and Edward Hopper have painted in Gloucester's exquisite light. The artists' association is the oldest art colony in constant operation in America.

Contents

Faneuil Hall originally operated as a marketplace and a meetinghouse, in the turbulent days before the American Revolution. Later, abolitionists and suffragists spoke here. Now, the hall forms part of the Boston National Historical Park, on the Freedom Trail. Shown are hundreds of new citizens taking their oath of allegiance.

The Boston Landmarks Orchestra plays in Trinity Church for First Night, Boston, *a city-wide celebration of the arts on New Year's Eve. The event sponsors hundreds of entertainers and is enjoyed by a million spectators annually.* First Night, Boston *was the original celebration of its kind and has inspired hundreds of similar events around the world.*

Christopher Columbus Waterfront Park has a fine view of the Boston skyline. In summer, the park offers free jazz concerts, art shows, and access to harbor island cruises. Waterfront Park, between Boston's North End and Quincy Market, provides a convenient spot to relax between forays to area shops and restaurants.

Above: *Elite runners from all over the world compete in the Boston Marathon. After twenty miles, they struggle up the infamous Heartbreak Hill, the last dreaded obstacle. Crowds cheer each competitor along the entire twenty-six-mile route from the start in Hopkinton to the finish line near Boston's Copley Square.*

Left: Tortoise and Hare *in Copley Square pays tribute to all Boston Marathon runners. Its creator, Nancy Schön, casts whimsical bronze sculptures that are often based on children's stories. Schön also created the beloved* Make Way for Ducklings *sculpture in the Boston Public Garden.*

The Museum of Fine Arts was established in 1870, when several institutions combined their collections and opened them to the public. The museum displays wide-ranging exhibits of American and European art, including one of the world's most extensive collections of Monet paintings. Other extraordinary collections include Asian, Egyptian, and Classical art and a variety of contemporary works in many media.

The Robert Gould Shaw Memorial, a bas relief monument created by Augustus Saint-Gaudens, honors the Massachusetts 54th Regiment, the first recruitment of African American soldiers in the Civil War. Their heroic story was featured in the movie Glory.

The Leonard P. Zakim Bunker Hill Bridge is a contemporary landmark on the Boston skyline. Its two towers reflect the shape of the nearby Bunker Hill Monument and its broad deck brings vehicles into the city in a flash. Before it opened to automobiles, the bridge hosted pedestrians twice and drew over a million participants.

Fenway Park is America's oldest major league baseball park. This intimate stadium has hosted many hall-of-famers, including Cy Young, Babe Ruth, Ted Williams, and Carl Yastrzemski. Red Sox fans, who loyally supported their team through an eighty-six-year drought, were finally rewarded in 2004 when the team broke "the curse of the Bambino" and won the World Series.

The Boston Pops orchestra performs at the annual Fourth of July concert in the Hatch Shell on the Charles River Esplanade. The event attracts millions of spectators every year, many of whom wait in line for hours to claim a spot on the lawn.

Quaint Beacon Hill, developed in the 1790s, features narrow streets and gaslights. Its preserved brick homes and cobbled lanes are antique treasures valued for their architectural integrity. Picturesque Acorn Street, shown here, is a private way; residents say that if the city owned it, the street would have been paved long ago.

Originally, Back Bay was a tidal marsh surrounding the Shawmut peninsula. As Boston grew, the wetland was filled in, creating wide Parisian boulevards lined with fashionable brick mansions. Wealthy families moved from crowded Beacon Hill to Back Bay, prime real estate then and now.

Boston Light, America's oldest lighthouse, highlights the Boston Harbor Islands National Recreation Area, accessible by ferry from downtown docks. In the harbor, visitors can explore a Civil War–era fort on Georges Island, pick berries on Thompson Island, camp on Peddocks Island, and enjoy scenic sunset cruises.

Above: *Commissioned in 1797, the* USS Constitution *was nicknamed Old Ironsides during the War of 1812, after enemy cannonballs bounced off its two-foot-thick oak hull. Every year, the* Constitution *cruises Boston Harbor and receives a twenty-one-gun salute on the Fourth of July.*

Left: *On Patriots' Day, Minuteman National Historical Park re-creates the first battles of the Revolutionary War. The events draw hundreds of colonial reenactors and thousands of spectators along the route taken by the British in their retreat from Concord and Lexington.*

Only six years after settling in Boston, the Puritans began to set aside money for a college for young men. They chose a site in Massachusetts Bay Colony's capital, Newtowne. Now Newtowne is Cambridge, the college is Harvard University, and commencement finds co-ed graduates making their way through busy Harvard Square.

Harvard University surrounds Harvard Square, a meeting place for an eclectic mix of students, protestors, shoppers, and tourists. Sidewalk cafés provide the perfect venues for people-watching, and kiosks direct sightseers to points of interest.

Architect Frank O. Gehry designed the Massachusetts Institute of Technology's Ray and Maria Stata Center as a hub for information sciences. The sleek metal façade and jutting angles serve as a counterpoint to the school's traditional granite-domed halls, just blocks away.

Facing page: *Mid-nineteenth-century Concord served as a focal point of literary talent. The Wayside, now part of the Minuteman National Historical Park, was at various times the home of authors Louisa May Alcott, Nathaniel Hawthorne, and Margaret Sidney.*

Above: *When Henry David Thoreau retreated to Walden Pond in 1845, it was "to live deliberately, to front only the essential facts of life." His diary from that time became the transcendentalist masterpiece,* Walden. *This one-room house replicates the one he built for about twenty-six dollars.*

Today, Walden Pond is a national historic landmark, and many consider it the birthplace of the conservation movement. The pond and its oak woodlands are preserved by the Massachusetts Department of Conservation and Recreation for fishing, swimming, and contemplative walks.

SALEM WITCH MUSEUM

OPEN
DAILY
10AM–7PM

Crane Beach, preserved by The Trustees of Reservations, was once part of the estate of Richard T. Crane, a Chicago industrialist. Today, its twelve hundred acres of beach and dunes provide nesting sites for the threatened piping plover, which lives in close proximity to beachgoers.

The statue Man at the Wheel, *by Gloucester artist Leonard Craske, honors that city's fishing community. Its inscription quotes Psalm 107: "They that go down to the sea in ships, that do business in great waters; these see the works of the Lord."*

The mouth of the Merrimack River was the home of the Newburyport Privateers, licensed pirates who attacked British vessels during the Revolution and the War of 1812. Their success brought wealth to them and defeat to the enemy. Ironically, Congress later needed to protect its own shipping revenues from the Privateers and built the first cutter, a forerunner of the United States Coast Guard, in Newburyport.

Facing page: *Salem's Turner-Ingersoll Mansion, better known as the House of the Seven Gables, was made famous in Nathaniel Hawthorne's 1851 novel of the same name. This interesting museum also includes the house next door, where Hawthorne was born.*

Above: *The city of Salem built America's first living-history museum, Salem 1630: Pioneer Village, to commemorate the three hundredth anniversary of the arrival of Governor John Winthrop and the Charter of the Massachusetts Bay Colony. Visitors watch demonstrations of daily life, militia drills, and seventeenth-century craftspeople at work.*

This picturesque fishing shack in Rockport has become the symbol of the town. Given the title "Motif #1" by painter Lester George Hornby, it appears in hundreds of works of art and is recognized all over the world. The shack was destroyed by the notorious blizzard of 1978 and rebuilt by the town within one year.

A trip to Bearskin Neck—a tiny peninsula lined with quaint little studios, shops, and restaurants—highlights a visit to Rockport. Tourists stroll its narrow streets and watch artists painting scenes of the nearby harbor and beaches. Lobstermen still haul their catch to its wharves and kayak tours embark from its shoreline.

In 1916, Ipswich cook Lawrence Woodman tried a new recipe and invented the fried clam. Now Woodman's is the leading clam shack on the North Shore. The restaurant offers a selection of seafood, including cooked lobsters ready to go.

Wingaersheek Beach in Gloucester counts among Cape Ann's most beautiful beaches. Situated between the Annisquam River and Ipswich Bay, it offers white sand, clear water, and huge rocks to play on. At low tide, the beach seems to go on forever.

In 1991, the Coast Guard announced plans to sell Eastern Point Lighthouse. After much fundraising and lobbying, the Lighthouse Preservation Society and area lighthouse lovers convinced the government to reverse its position. The light guards the entrance to Gloucester Harbor and appears in paintings by Winslow Homer and Fitzhugh Lane.

Gloucester serves as one of Massachusetts' major fishing ports, home of the Gorton fisherman and anchorage of the ship Andrea Gail, *featured in the movie* The Perfect Storm. *Commercial fishing accounts for about 15 percent of Gloucester's economy.*

The Peabody Essex Museum in Salem showcases two hundred years of international art, architecture, and culture. Its collections include more than one million pieces of maritime art and cultural exhibits from New England, Asia, Africa, and the Pacific Islands.

The ship Friendship *replicates a Salem merchant vessel used on trade routes to Europe, Asia, and the Spice Islands (now Indonesia). The Salem Maritime National Historical Site preserves the* Friendship *and twelve historic buildings that chronicle the role of seafaring trade in establishing the economic independence of the young United States.*

The city of Lowell developed around a mile-long complex of textile mills. At the Lowell National Historical Park, visitors can walk or take trolleys from the visitor center to the Boott Cotton Mill and to exhibits demonstrating the canals and turbines that powered the historic mills.

The Lowell Folk Festival presents three days of music, dancing, parades, and international foods. It is America's biggest free folk fest, a spin-off of the roving National Folk Festival. Here, crowds gather for a concert at Bourdinghouse Square, once home to the Lowell "mill girls" and immigrant laborers.

Ipswich is an equestrian center, with many bridle paths winding through woods and fields. Here, riders from Keough Stables enjoy a winter ride with their horses on Crane Beach, a property of The Trustees of Reservations.

Lowell National Historical Park rangers open a lock on the Pawtucket Canal for a tour boat. Added to the two local rivers, the canals were built to bring water power to the mills, transforming Lowell into a city of islands.

When Marblehead Light's beacon stopped working during the infamous hurricane of 1938, the keeper used his car battery to fuel the light. The tower's distinctive skeleton raises the beacon high above scenic Marblehead Harbor, welcoming sailboats and fishing vessels.

The Parker River National Wildlife Refuge in Newburyport welcomes hikers, bikers, and sunbathers to its paths and beaches. However, the refuge is best known for its wide variety of avian species and is listed as one of the nation's top ten bird-watching spots.

Chapter 3

South of Boston

Heritage

When Chief Massasoit walked the Plymouth pinelands, the forests and rivers provided ample food for his people, the Wampanoag. When a group of Pilgrims settled in the Plymouth Colony in 1620, Massasoit hoped they could live with each other. The natives taught the newcomers to grow crops in their adopted home, and the Pilgrims brought modern goods to trade for beaver pelts.

As time went by, Massasoit and his son Metacomet saw their land appropriated and food stocks depleted by an ever-increasing number of colonists. By the time Metacomet, known as King Philip,

waged war against the white settlers, there were too many to overcome. However, there were a few friends—men like innkeeper James Cole, who came to Plymouth in 1633, and his son Hugh. When two of Hugh's sons were captured in a raid, Metacomet ordered them released because of his respect for their father.

James and Hugh Cole, my ancestors, were freemen in Plymouth Colony. Their way of life is now vividly recreated at Plimoth Plantation, the region's premier living-history museum, where costumed docents immerse themselves in seventeenth-century traditions. For people tracing their genealogy, the many historical museums south of Boston fill out details of the daily lives of ancestors merely sketched in town records. In my own family research, I have found seamen, farmers, shipwrights, engineers, soldiers, and skilled craftsmen. In fact, my great-grandfather Edward R. Cole was chronicled as the last shipsmith to forge harpoons for New Bedford whalers.

New Bedford was the epicenter of the whaling trade. It was here that young Herman Melville boarded the whaler Acushnet in 1841, living the greatest adventure of his life and inspiring his classic book *Moby-Dick*. At the height of the whaling era, New Bedford's bustling waterfront swarmed with sailors and tradesmen from all over the world. This period is described by the staff at the New Bedford Whaling National Historical Park and reflected in the cobbled streets and elegant architecture: the

Facing page: *The* Mayflower II *recreates the vessel that carried more than a hundred Pilgrims across the Atlantic. They spent seven months on the tiny ship, which measured only 25 feet wide and 106 feet long. Visitors can talk with costumed role players who recount their characters' experiences on the difficult voyage.*

Above: *Battleship Cove in Fall River pays tribute to World War II's mighty naval vessels. Visitors can explore the decks of the USS* Massachusetts, *imagine diving deep on the submarine* Lionfish, *and man the guns on* Big Mamie. *The nearby Fall River Heritage State Park and the Fall River Marine Museum, with* Titanic *artifacts, fill out a day's tour.*

imposing customs house, the numerous sea captains' mansions, and the preserved warehouses now serving as artists' spaces.

Just west of New Bedford, Fall River was established as a premier factory city, with more than fifty huge granite mill buildings lining the Quequechan River. More recently, the city has been reinvented as the birthplace of factory-outlet shopping. The nearby South Coast is primarily an idyllic backwater of former shipbuilding villages and saltwater farms bounded by hand-laid stone walls. Behind this coastal fringe are suburban communities connected by major highways that radiate from Boston like the spokes of a wheel.

But southeastern Massachusetts is more than cities and towns. Some of the wilderness revered by Massasoit has been preserved for us. Thousands of acres of salt marsh, beach, and forest are set aside as state parks and conservation areas. Come explore. With so many attractions so close to major cities, there's something here for everyone.

Plimoth Plantation is a living-history museum that re-creates life in colonial America. Costumed role players assume the personality and background of members of the Pilgrim colony as if it were still 1627. A favorite game of visitors is to try to make the guides acknowledge events later than the seventeenth century.

The buildings at Plimoth Plantation are constructed of local materials, assembled using the same techniques as the original colonial homes. The museum also breeds period livestock, completing the aura of authenticity.

A harvester collects cranberries, first cultivated in 1816, at the Cranberry Festival in Carver. Growers flood low-lying bogs at harvest time, so the fruit can be skimmed off the surface of the water—just in time to embellish Thanksgiving dinner.

In the first half of the nineteenth century, the whaling industry centered around New Bedford. Its harbor swarmed with seamen and tradesmen from all over the world, and maritime businesses lined its cobblestone streets.

The Rotch-Jones-Duff House was built by New Bedford merchant William Rotch Junior in 1834. It was the height of the whaling era, when wealthy families lined County Street with stylish mansions. A magnificent formal rose garden now surrounds the house museum, and fine period furniture fills its rooms.

The New Bedford Whaling National Historical Park was established in 1996 to preserve the city's rich seafaring heritage. The park sparked a rebirth of the waterfront district, and today the area is full of artists, craftspeople, and tourists.

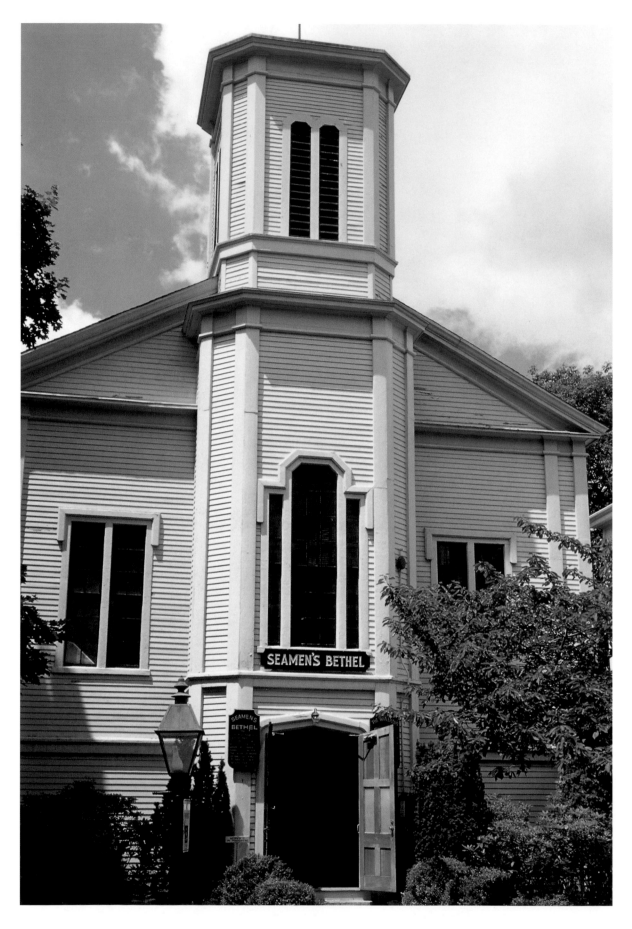

The Seamen's Bethel, now part of the New Bedford Whaling National Historical Park, provided spiritual comfort to sailors far from home. Herman Melville attended services there before shipping out on the Acushnet and later wrote about it in his novel Moby-Dick.

The Trustees of Reservations' Slocum's River Reserve in Dartmouth preserves the character of the area's traditional saltwater farms. Hand-built stone walls divide pastures, which extend down to the river's edge.

The New Bedford Whaling Museum displays collections of maritime objects including the Lagoda, *a half-size replica of a square-rigged whaling ship. KOBO (King of the Blue Ocean), a juvenile blue whale skeleton, hangs over the lobby.*

The tidal flats of Westport Point make rich nurseries for shellfish. Clams harvested in these waters are called quahogs (pronounced KO-hogs). Locals prepare them by stuffing the shells with a zesty mixture of chopped clams, bread, and Portuguese spices.

New Bedford's Greek and Portuguese population has a long seafaring heritage. The city's fishing haul is the largest in the nation, bringing in nearly two hundred million dollars worth of fresh seafood annually.

The Blessing of the Fleet, part of the New Bedford Summerfest, draws both traditional fishing crews and modern yachtsmen. Priests sprinkle holy water from the deck of one of the many cruise ships that now make the city a port-of-call.

At the end of the nineteenth century, resort communities sprang up around Boston, and city-dwellers arrived via trolley to bask in the sunshine and breathe sea air. Attractions such as this elegant hand-carved carousel at Paragon Park in Hull won many admirers. The Massachusetts Department of Conservation and Recreation now protects Nantasket Beach Reservation and its beautiful carousel.

Copicut Woods, a property of The Trustees of Reservations, provides access to the Southeastern Massachusetts Bioreserve, a 13,600-acre swath of forest in Fall River, Freetown, and Dartmouth. Copicut features a deserted farm with streams and woods punctuated by stone walls. Here, the forest floor wears a cloak of ferns

During the War of 1812, a British ship threatened Scituate Harbor. The lighthouse keeper's two teenage daughters, home alone, doused the light and played a fife and drum to mimic the local militia. The British left in haste, and the "American Army of Two" is remembered at the annual Scituate Days.

New England is known for its lobsters, crustaceans that come to the table boiled, baked, stuffed, or tucked in a pie. First-timers are often surprised to be presented with a whole lobster and tools to crack open its claws and tail. The work is worth the effort!

Westport Point is one of several quiet ports on the South Coast, an area where the land slopes gradually to the sea. Broad rivers and inlets provide anchorage for lobstermen and sailors.

The Westport Rivers Winery planted its first vines in 1986. Five years later, the Russell family was producing twelve hundred cases of white and rosé wines per year. This South Coast vineyard is now one of the premiere sparkling-wine producers in the East. Visitors can tour the vineyard and sample its offerings.

*Rosebay rhododendron (*Rhododendron maximum*) once grew wild throughout the Northeast but is now rare. This grove is protected by The Trustees of Reservations in a private site known as the Medfield Rhododendrons. The light pink flowers bloom around the middle of June.*

World's End, originally the estate of businessman John Brewer, is now a property of The Trustees of Reservations. Brewer commissioned famed landscape architect Frederick Law Olmsted to showcase the peninsula's views of Boston Harbor.

Horseneck Beach State Reservation in Westport comprises almost six hundred acres of barrier beach and salt marsh. The park is popular with wind surfers and swimmers and hosts many species of birds. Campers at Horseneck enjoy the constant breezes of Gooseberry Neck, a sandy spit surrounded by water on three sides.

Allens Pond, a Massachusetts Audubon Society sanctuary in Dartmouth, marks the first New England landfall for many migratory birds. The sanctuary preserves a small crescent beach and acres of salt marsh along Buzzards Bay.

Chapter 4

Cape Cod and the Islands

Timeless

Since the last glacier finished creating Cape Cod and the islands of Nantucket and Martha's Vineyard, not much seems to have changed here. Sure, the sea has undercut cliffs and broken through barrier beaches. Certainly, the land has been traversed by Wampanoag hunters, Pilgrim farmers, Portuguese fishermen, African American whalers, Methodist preachers, and countless tourists. And, of course, industries have come and gone, modes of transportation have waxed and waned, and maps have been revised dozens of times. Even so, this place has a timeless quality, a sense that if you walk

a few hundred feet from any road, you will still see vistas enjoyed by the first humans who came to hunt and fish.

Cape residents have always reaped the bounty of the land and sea. Farming, fishing, salt-making, whaling, tourism—each occupation has taken its turn as a source of income. But humans have never truly tamed the land. The ocean rules here. A winter walk on Nauset Beach can be a wild affair, and a spring stroll through Truro's pine barrens sounds as it must have thousands of years ago—footsteps muffled in a soft carpet of pine needles, the air full of bird song. Timeless.

The area's man-made elements seem ageless, too. The whole town of Nantucket has been designated a national historic landmark, with more than eight hundred buildings constructed before 1850. Locals refer to places like Cotuit and Centerville—names of old villages, now part of the town of Barnstable. Lighthouses and windmills are preserved and appreciated. This widespread esteem for historical integrity gives the region an enduring air.

In recent times, the region has become increasingly popular. Steamships and railroads carried nineteenth-century summer visitors and conveyed materials to build fashionable mansions. The Cape Cod Canal brought recreational boaters. Bridges and

Facing page: *At the tip of Cape Cod, the community of Provincetown has a predominantly Portuguese heritage. Boats leave port before sunrise and return in late afternoon, in time to bring fresh seafood to local restaurants for the evening meal.*

Above: *The Atlantic Ocean has created a series of steep cliffs at White Crest Beach on Cape Cod's eastern coast. Stiff winds and pounding waves make the area popular with both surfers and windsurfers.*

highways opened the area to millions of weekenders. And many who have come for a visit want to stay. The cape and islands, with their mild climate and abundance of charms, draw tourists and "washashores," or permanent immigrants.

The attractions are many—the most obvious, miles of gorgeous white beaches. Quaint villages boast historic inns and country stores. Natural areas entice hikers and bikers, anglers and paddlers. Events abound, from the Martha's Vineyard Agricultural Fair to Eastham's Windmill Weekend to Cape-League baseball games. Golfers and mini-golfers are well-served by area courses.

Shoppers comb boutiques in Edgartown, Nantucket, and Chatham. Collectors flock to Brewster's Antique Alley. Provincetown's bohemian street scene and colorful nightlife attract artists and lovers. Museums preserve the past, display local art, and interpret natural history. And the performing arts thrive—in playhouses, film festivals, and musical venues.

Yes, change is constant here, driven by the tides and time and by human progress. The people who live here adapt. Orleans fishermen become charter boat captains, Eastham cottage colonies become condos, and Outer Cape resorts cater to the needs of a changing clientele. Island populations swell in summer and ebb in winter. Storms, both meteorological and cultural, sweep the region. But Cape Cod and the islands remain essentially changeless—seaside havens for all.

The Old Harbor Museum chronicles the history of the U.S. Life Saving Service, charged with rescuing passengers and crew shipwrecked at Race Point. The museum is part of the Cape Cod National Seashore.

Sandy Neck is a popular natural area on Cape Cod Bay. Sunbathers enjoy the town beach, and RV campers roll out of bed to cast lines for bluefish and striped bass. Behind the beachfront, the Nature Conservancy protects a large area of dunes and heath, open to hikers.

The Heritage Museums and Gardens in Sandwich preserve Cape Cod's cultural legacy. Exhibits include Josiah Lilly III's collection of vintage cars housed in a round Shaker barn. In June, the grounds' seventy-six acres of Dexter rhododendrons are spectacular, and in July and August, the daylilies are stunning.

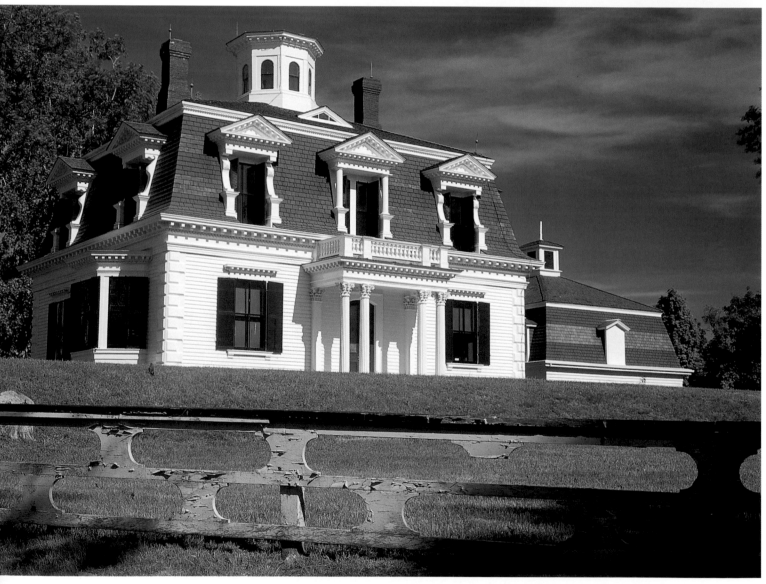

Edward Penniman first went to sea when he was eleven and eventually became an extraordinarily successful whaling captain. His wife, "Gustie," accompanied him on three whaling voyages before they retired to this elegant mansion in 1868. The Cape Cod National Seashore now preserves the Captain Edward Penniman house for future generations.

Although Cape Cod has many antique shops, the King's Highway in Brewster has such a high concentration of them that it is known as Antique Alley.

The 1791 Judah Baker Windmill in Yarmouth overlooks the Bass River. Early sketches of Cape Cod show clusters of windmills pumping brine into huge pans to make salt. They were also used to grind corn and wheat into flour.

The Army Corps of Engineers built the Cape Cod Canal in 1914 to cut the distance between Boston and New York. Two award-winning bridges span the canal, bringing thirty-four million cars to the Cape annually.

The watercourse that powers the Stoney Brook Mill in Brewster acts as a spring-time highway for migrating alewives, or herring. In the summer, the gristmill still grinds corn, and in the fall, the millpond reflects the colorful foliage.

Cape Codders go camping at Nickerson State Park in Brewster. Its expansive oak and pine forest contains several camping loops with more than four hundred sites, including some with yurts. Nickerson also features trout fishing in eight stocked kettle ponds and miles of hiking trails and bike paths that connect the park to the Cape Cod Rail Trail.

When Europeans first explored the Cape, they described forests having many types of trees. Settlers cleared the land, and today only a few species survive: scrub oak, pitch pine, and this group of Atlantic white cedars in the Cape Cod National Seashore.

The little lighthouse at Brant Point, Nantucket, has been rebuilt seven times and, today, stands as a much-loved greeting for ferry passengers. Its decoration each April for the Daffodil Festival signals the arrival of spring.

Ferries embark from Hyannis, one of the area's busiest harbors, to the islands of Nantucket and Martha's Vineyard. Visitors can also experience a pirate cruise, a schooner ride, or a harbor tour that offers a glimpse of the Kennedy compound, and then satisfy their appetites with waterfront alfresco dining.

Nantucket celebrates Christmas with a month-long festival called Nantucket Noel, culminating in the Nantucket Stroll. Here, carolers spread holiday cheer on Centre Street, where Quaker women once ran the shops while their husbands were at sea.

Above: *Quaint country stores like this one in Centerville contribute to the rustic atmosphere of the Cape. Note the separate benches for Democrats and Republicans—a sign that politics have always engendered splits, but not divisions, of the people.*

Right: *At the 1903 Green Briar Jam Kitchen in East Sandwich, staff members from the Thornton W. Burgess Society make a mouthwatering array of preserves the old-fashioned way. Burgess authored the* Brer Rabbit *children's books.*

Above: *In 1835, nine Edgartown men retreated to the wilderness to pray for enlightenment. Their revival camp at Oak Bluffs grew into a colony of gingerbread cottages, now a haven of serenity in a bustling tourist town.*

The old fishing village of Siasconset ("S'conset") lies on Nantucket's east shore. Its cluster of shingled cottages, once tiny fishing shacks, are now covered with roses. The village is a favorite destination of Nantucket bicyclists.

The boulders and bright clay cliffs at Aquinnah, on Martha's Vineyard, formed over twenty-five thousand years ago when the Wisconsin Stage glacier plowed vast amounts of sand and rock through New England. The same glacial process also created Cape Cod and Nantucket.

Artist Eleanor Norcross, inspired by the potential of small rural museums to foster a love of art, founded the Fitchburg Art Museum in 1925. To start the museum, she bequeathed her personal collection of Islamic, Asian, and European art, as well as some of her own works.

Historic Deerfield, a museum and national historic landmark, includes a collection of eighteenth- and nineteenth-century homes built when the Pioneer Valley represented America's frontier. This unspoiled New England village is surrounded by traditional farms.

Above: *Hot air balloons launch at sunrise during the annual Green River Festival in Greenfield. The festival is over twenty years old and features a weekend of crafts, food, games, magic, and music in the Berkshire foothills.*

Right: *Springfield's Eastern States Exposition— "The Big E"—exemplifies an old-fashioned trade fair that demonstrates new technology and products, as well as providing amusements and novelties to attract the crowds.*

At an encampment in Historic Deerfield, Silver Bear, a Mohawk dancer, commemorates the 1704 raid on the settlement during Queen Anne's War. The museum offers educational facilities and events to foster understanding of eighteenth-century life.

Mount Holyoke College was founded in 1837 as the Mount Holyoke Female Seminary. It taught the daughters of a growing middle class to "Go where no one else will go." The first graduating classes contained future teachers, missionaries, and some of the first female doctors in America.

Holyoke Heritage State Park recalls that city's industrial heyday. At Hadley Falls, industrialists built canals and mills that produced much of the world's fine writing paper, giving Holyoke the title "Paper City."

Spring wildflowers decorate the forest floor of J. A. Skinner State Park, and bright foliage adorns its slopes in fall. Here a red trillium, or wake-robin, soaks up the spring sunshine.

Visitors access J. A. Skinner State Park, on Mount Holyoke in Hadley, by road in warm weather and by foot year-round. A nearby view of the Connecticut River oxbow was immortalized in a painting by Thomas Cole of the Hudson School.

The city of Leominster, birthplace of Johnny Appleseed, maintains Sholan Farms as the last working apple orchard within its limits. The farm hosts many popular events, including the Apple Blossom Festival in May and the Scarecrow Festival in October.

This white pine grove in Erving State Forest was probably planted after the hurricane of 1938 blew down most of the area's hardwood forest. In June, the forest's woodland trails are resplendent with mountain laurel blossoms.

Above: *Lovely Laurel Lake, in Erving State Forest, offers a peaceful retreat in north-central Massachusetts. Recreational opportunities include swimming, boating, fishing, hiking, horseback riding, and winter sports.*

Left: *The Middle Branch of the Swift River tumbles through a granite gorge at Bears Den, preserved by The Trustees of Reservations. Invisible from the road, the falls can be reached by following a short path through a cool, dense hemlock forest.*

Chapter 6

The West

A Cultural Retreat

Sometimes western Massachusetts seems a million miles from Boston. The distance is more than geographic. It's cultural. A gracious ambience pervades the area, drawing city weekenders searching for a rural retreat.

The region is a patchwork of farms and forests, dotted with tiny villages and crisscrossed by small roads. But ah, what roads they are! High roads, where morning sunlight streaks across meadows steaming with dew and edged with maples. Low roads, intertwined with tumultuous brooks running beneath massive hemlocks. Roads to farmsteads through covered bridges spanning sparkling rivers that drain unbroken forests. These roads are not for hurrying but for leisurely exploration.

One of these thoroughfares, the Mohawk Trail, is a wild, serpentine coaster ride over the Hoosac Mountain Range to the Berkshires, culminating in a hairpin turn with a scenic view. The highway is punctuated with kitschy throwbacks to '50s automobile culture: American Indian–themed souvenir shops, lookout platforms boasting three-state views, and various "summit" houses and restaurants. The Mohawk Trail is especially popular in autumn, when thousands of visitors enjoy the brilliant foliage.

In the Hampshire County hill towns, you can browse in country stores, shop for antiques, or visit artisan galleries. Outdoor enthusiasts enjoy whitewater rafting on the Deerfield River and hiking with llamas. Late summer brings a collection of country fairs, and in autumn, this is the place to find fresh produce at a farm stand or just the right pumpkin for your front porch.

The Berkshires have long been billed as "America's premier cultural resort." Tanglewood and the Jacobs Pillow Dance Festival highlight the performing arts. The region has several notable art museums, including Norman Rockwell's studio and the

Facing page: *Wildflowers in Hop Brook Wildlife Management Area attract birds and wildlife. The wet meadow sits between two ridges in the Berkshire foothills and provides a fine view of Tyringham Cobble, a popular hiking spot on the Appalachian Trail.*

Above: *Spanning the Housatonic River, the Sheffield covered bridge was rebuilt to replace the state's oldest covered bridge after it was destroyed by fire. Massachusetts natives excelled in this industry. Timothy Palmer designed America's first covered bridge, and the Howe family built many of New England's covered bridges.*

Massachusetts Museum of Contemporary Art, a former factory transformed into a breathtaking space for exhibits. You can experience Victorian luxury at fabulous summer "cottages" like the Mount or pamper yourself at a day spa.

Much of the area between the Mohawk Trail and the Massachusetts Turnpike remains forested and preserved. Among the more than thirty state parks and forests west of the Connecticut River are Clarksburg, with its spectacular views of fall foliage; Bash Bish Falls, an easy hike; and Savoy Mountain, with lakeside campsites and rental log cabins. The Westfield River has been designated "wild and scenic" by the U.S. Department of the Interior, and its waters are enjoyed by anglers and floaters. There are even stands of virgin forest hidden in the mountains. And many private preserves offer opportunities to explore the area's natural heritage.

It's the diversity of recreational opportunities that makes western Massachusetts so appealing. Where else can you wet a line at dawn, bike over back roads to pick your own berries, attend a jazz concert, relax in a romantic B&B, shop for antiques and visit your choice of museums, all in one weekend? Yes, the tranquil towns of western Massachusetts seem a million miles from hectic Boston. But you can get there in just two hours.

Jacob's Pillow in Becket was founded in 1932 by renowned dancer Ted Shawn and grew into a leading dance institution. In addition to performances, Jacob's Pillow hosts a school of dance, intern programs, and two theaters. This popular Inside/Out *presentation features dancers in an open-air setting of spectacular mountain beauty.*

The Mount Greylock State Reservation crowns the Nature Conservancy's Berkshire Taconic Landscape. Lookout points along its scenic byway afford magnificent mountain vistas. On clear days, the view extends to Vermont, New Hampshire, and New York.

A Mohawk lifts his arms to the Great Spirit in the monument Hail To The Sunrise. *The monument commemorates the Native American tribes that lived on the Mohawk Trail. An adjacent pool is surrounded by one hundred stones inscribed by nationwide tribes.*

The Mohawk Trail was built along an old Native American route to bring travelers from Boston to New York. This hairpin turn, a landmark viewpoint with a restaurant, is required to negotiate the steep western slope of the Hoosac Range.

The Big Indian gift shop invites travelers to browse for moccasins and explore its petting zoo. Many kitschy attractions dotted the Mohawk Trail in the early twentieth century when scenic highways were first built and Americans took to them in affordable automobiles.

Above: *Boston sculptor Sir Henry Kitson designed this gingerbread house, called Santarella, as an artist's studio. Kitson also created the statue* Minuteman *at Lexington and Salem's* Roger Conant *statue. Santarella, located in Tyringham, has served as a museum and an art gallery and is being restored for private functions.*

Right: *Brilliant fall foliage surrounds a pond in Savoy Mountain State Forest. Campers can settle into a cozy log cabin or pitch a tent in a fragrant apple orchard. Popular activities include hiking, fishing, horseback riding, snowmobiling, and cross-country skiing. This remote park also boasts a spectacular waterfall and a natural bog.*

Over five hundred plant varieties—and a labor of love by the local women's club—have transformed an old trolley bridge into a lush public garden. The unique Shelburne Falls Bridge of Flowers, in bloom from April through October, attracts thousands of visitors each year to the four-hundred-foot span of fragrance and color.

Sixty-three buildings in Williamsburg are listed on the National Historic Register, including the Williamsburg General Store. A landmark for over one hundred years, the emporium still stocks homemade baked goods, "real" ice cream, penny candies, and aged cheese. Shoppers bring home a taste of yesterday.

Right: *The Tanglewood Music Center, summer home of the Boston Symphony Orchestra, attracts more than three hundred thousand music-lovers each year. This simple shed was built in 1937 to protect patrons from bad weather; on sunny days, they picnic on the surrounding lawn as symphonic strains waft through the trees on summer breezes.*

Below: *The round stone barn in Hancock Shaker Village is a masterpiece of utilitarian design. The village, a living-history museum, recalls a way of life that devoted "hands to work, heart to God." The Hancock community was once home to three hundred members and renowned for its botanical and household products.*

Visitors to Otis Reservoir can sail its clean waters, ski behind a power boat, or kayak quiet coves perfumed with water lilies. Campers and RVers can roast marshmallows in private campgrounds or sleep under the stars in Tolland State Forest, and anglers reel in trout, salmon, and smallmouth bass from their own secret spots.

Rockwell's studio at the Norman Rockwell Museum offers a offers a glimpse of the famous painter's working environment. Preserved as he left it, the studio contains his equipment, travel souvenirs, and his personal library of art books. Rockwell first worked behind his house in downtown Stockbridge; he moved the studio building to this location in 1986.

MASS MoCA, the Massachusetts Museum of Contemporary Art, features cutting-edge art that aims to connect the creator and the space with the audience. Exhibits include work in all media, set in a massive converted mill with vast rooms and soaring ceilings. Shown is Proposition Player, by Matthew Ritchie.

In 1793, Williams College was established by Colonel Ephraim Williams, who dreamed that a school and a comfortable community would replace the frontier military outpost in Williamstown. Over the centuries, the curriculum has expanded and the student population grown more diverse, but the college still challenges students "to dare, to do, and to suffer."

Picturesque Williamstown is known as "the Village Beautiful" because of its scenic setting and unspoiled Main Street. It is surrounded by farmland and the Berkshire hills, just south of the Vermont border.

The Mount, in Lenox, was built by Edith Wharton, the first woman writer to win the Pulitzer Prize for fiction. She designed the estate to support her lifestyle and her art. Wharton's nonfiction works deal with architecture, landscape, interior design, and travel.

Left: *The waters of Bash Bish Falls begin high in Mount Washington State Forest and tumble into a pool at the bottom of a deep, winding gorge. In the mid-nineteenth century, the picturesque falls became one of the most visited destinations in the Berkshire Mountains.*

Above: *The white rock of the marble arch in Natural Bridge State Park formed millions of years ago, during the Paleozoic Era. Many buildings in the North Adams area contain marble quarried here. In the summer, park interpreters explain the natural forces that created the arch.*

Writers Herman Melville and Nathaniel Hawthorne became friends on a hike up Monument Mountain, now owned by The Trustees of Reservations. Their meeting is celebrated annually when members of the Herman Melville Society hike to the summit and read from his works.

The rambling farmhouse called Arrowhead housed Herman Melville and his family from 1850 to 1863. The view of Mount Greylock from his study window was said to be the author's inspiration for the white whale in Moby-Dick, *and descriptions of the area appear in many of his works.*

The mountainous western border of Massachusetts once acted as a barrier to westward migration. Here, seen from Stony Ledge on Mount Greylock, it offers an inspiring view of unbroken forest, where stands of old-growth hemlocks rise majestically from the valleys.

About the Author/Photographer

(Photograph © Gary M. Blazon)

Susan Cole Kelly specializes in photographing the beauty of New England with intimate details of nature, people, and places. A Massachusetts native, she majored in art at the University of New Hampshire, studied photography at the New England School of Photography, and took master's classes at the Maine Photographic Workshops.

Kelly has previously photographed three books: *Our Boston* (Voyageur Press, 1998), *Lighthouses of New England* (Voyageur Press, 2001), and *The Complete Illustrated Guide to Boston's Public Parks and Gardens* (Silver Lining Books, 2002). She has contributed to the *Audubon Guide to New England*, *National Geographic Society Guide to Birdwatching*, and *Cape Cod on my Mind* and provided several cover images for Countryman Press' *Explorers Guide* series.

A regular contributor to *New England Travel & Life*, Kelly has also illustrated articles for *Vermont Life*, *Downeast*, *Yankee*, *Cape Cod Life*, and the *Cape Cod Travel Guide*. Her photographs have been featured in wall calendars, postcards, and engagement calendars, including several exclusive titles published annually by Browntrout Publishers.

Susan Cole Kelly is a member of the North American Nature Photographers Association and makes her home in Boston's historic North End.